YOUR KNOWLEDGE HAS VALUE

Bibliographic information published by the German National Library:

The German National Library lists this publication in the National Bibliography; detailed bibliographic data are available on the Internet at http://dnb.dnb.de .

Imprint:

Copyright © 2016 GRIN Verlag
Print and binding: Books on Demand GmbH, Norderstedt Germany
ISBN: 9783668899124

This book at GRIN:

https://www.grin.com/document/453346

Janine Bergmeir

How intersectionality is deployed in "12 years a slave"

GRIN Verlag

GRIN - Your knowledge has value

Since its foundation in 1998, GRIN has specialized in publishing academic texts by students, college teachers and other academics as e-book and printed book. The website www.grin.com is an ideal platform for presenting term papers, final papers, scientific essays, dissertations and specialist books.

Visit us on the internet:

http://www.grin.com/

http://www.facebook.com/grincom

http://www.twitter.com/grin_com

Eberhard Karls Universität Tübingen

Philosophische Fakultät: Anglistik/Amerikanistik

HS: Marriage, Sex, Adultery: Gender relations in the 19th century

6. Fachsemester

An Intersectual Approach: How Intersectionality is deployed in 12 years a slave

Janine Bergmeir

Tübingen, den 30.09.2016

Content

1   Introduction 1

2   Intersectionality 3

   2.1   Constituent Parts of Intersectionality 4

     2.1.1   A Definition - Inter-sectional-ity...4

     2.1.2   Historical Background of Intersectionality...5

     2.1.3   Class, Race, Ethnicity and Gender..6

3   12 years a slave 8

   3.1   Historical background of 12 years a slave 8

     3.1.1   The American Pre - Civil War..8

4   12 years a slave – The Narrative of Solomon Northup 10

   4.1   Deploying intersectionality 10

     4.1.1   Mistress Epps – the green-eyed monster...10

     4.1.2   Patsey – the helpless bondwoman...12

     4.1.3   From white to black; from men to women and back - Bringing it together....14

5   12 years a slave – The Film...17

   5.1   Film style 18

   5.2   Music and Sound...20

   5.3   Camera Work 21

     5.3.1   The whipping...22

   5.4   Editing 23

   5.5   Art Direction..23

6   Conclusion: From Truthful Novel to Emotional Film 26

7   Works cited 28

1 Introduction

Slavery pertains to the woeful history of America as a calculated and colossal example of man's inhumanity to man. It is a grievous monument, full of hatred and brutality, about which stories emerged early. The slave history of America has produced many and various narratives. One of such stories was that of Solomon Northup who lived as a freeman in upstate New York and awoke to find himself in chains as a slave after he was drugged. He endured a slave-life in disparate Louisiana plantations until he was finally discovered by family and friends and found his way back into freedom. With the assistance of David Wilson, he published the book *12 Years a Slave: Narrative of Solomon Northup, a citizen of New-York, kidnapped in Washington city in 1841, and rescued in 1853, from a cotton plantation near the Red River in Louisiana* in 1853. In the 19th century, the book was a bestseller, but fell into obscurity until the 1960's. This was the time, when black legal scholar Kimberlé Crenshaw came up with the theory of intersectionality, and serves as the essence of this academic paper. In 2013, British filmmaker Steve McQueen has produced the film adaption of the slave narrative memoir *12 years a slave.*

In this academic work, I will examine two different responses to the issue of representing the brutal world of human beings bought, sold and used up like property in literature and film. I will analyze the novel *12 years a slave* and the film adaption of the same name in terms of Kimberlé Crenshaws theory of intersectionality and its constituents such as race, gender, ethnicity, and class which are defining dimensions of inequality in this context. The primary aim is to examine how various axes of the term construct one another and how inequalities are articulated and connected with differences between human beings. This will be done by illustrating the multidimensional character of the various axis of the intersectional perspective. "Through an awareness of intersectionality, we can better acknowledge and ground the differences among us" (Crenshaw).

In the second chapter I will commence with an overview on the term of intersectionality itself and the history of the emergence, followed by a definition of its components.

In the third chapter, concerned with the history, I will provide a short general introduction to 12 years a slave and its environment, in particular the pre-civil war and the history of slavery.

Subsequently, I will analyze how the approach of intersectionality in the narrative *12 years a slave* is implemented and becomes apparent through the two female characters Patsey and Mary Epps, who will be introduced in separate chapters. I will particularly focus on their treatment and how the context of slavery in the 19th century is employing the concept of intersectionality.

In the last part of my analysis, concerned with the film, I will illustrate how contrastive these two works are in their approaches to the delicate topic and I will provide a general introduction to the emotional approach the film bases itself on. Afterwards, I will analyze how this approach is implemented, and becomes apparent in terms of narration, camera work, composition, editing, music and sound, as well as art direction and film style. I will particularly focus on how the cinematic realization and its resulting effects differ from the approaches in Northup's memoir.

In the overall conclusion to this thesis, I will finally summarize my main arguments to illustrate the passage from truthful novel to emotional film.

2   Intersectionality

In the last three decades the term that started it all with feminist thoughts and its development, had been placed in a dock: Gender, seen as a social category on a single-axis, consisting of "female / women" and "male / men" began to lose its topicality when theorizing and struggling complex forms of social injustices. The construction of gender as a social category was more or less refused by feminists of color because they questioned the belonging of the term 'gender' with respect to women of color and the tendency of feminism to treat race and gender as reciprocal exclusive categories of analysis and experience. This two-edged criticism gave rise to 'intersectionality', as a fresh and new way of approaching multiple levels of subordination experienced by marginal groups of women, who apparently stood outside the idea of the primal image of women imagined by formerly feminists (white, efficient bodies, heterosexual and from the middle-class).

Black legal scholar Kimberlé Crenshaw coined the term intersectionality in her instructive 1989 essay namely *Demarginalizing the Intersection of Race and Sex: a Black Feminist Critique of Antidiscrimination Doctrine, Feminist Theory and Antiracist Politics* as a critical response to white feminists silence on African American women's oppression, the anti-racist movement and also for disregarding the needs of women on behalf of racial unity. Accordingly, she was concerned with the lack of appropriate support for women of color under the US judicial system. She argues that there is very hardly a correlation between anti-sexist politics and anti-racist approaches and that they rarely correspond to each other, negatively implicating the understanding of black women as subjects for feminist interference.

Crenshaw's most mentioned piece of work concerns primarily around women of color in the United States of America and evolved as a beneficial analytical method in feminist law. There are many other feminist scholars who found resonance in their own research that is concerned with different social contexts overall. However, what can be adopted and learned from Crenshaw's insight is that multiple axes of oppression exist, which are affecting and interacting with each other in considerable ways. The notion of the concept intersectionality is not an abstract or a complex one, but a genuine description of many-sided oppressions which are experienced. For clarifying the concept, Crenshaw used a comparison which is referring to a traffic intersection:

> Consider an analogy for traffic in an intersection, coming and going in all four directions. Discrimination, like traffic through an intersection, may flow in one

3

direction, and it may flow in another. If an accident happened in an intersection, it can be caused by cars travelling from any number of directions and,
sometimes, from all of them. Similarly, if a Black woman is harmed because
she is in the intersection, her injury could result from sex discrimination or
race discrimination. But it is not always easy to reconstruct an accident:
Sometimes the skid marks and the injuries simply indicate that they occurred
simultaneously, frustrating efforts to determine which driver caused the
harm.[4] (Crenshaw, 1989: 149).

What Crenshaw demonstrated is that projects, which are aiming at remedying the
subordination of racial or gender through a single axis, end up as universally male or
universally white. The insights of women of color, and other critical views about the
limits of equality, brought a critical race theory and added these understandings to
the principles of discrimination. In the United States but also in Europe, the term intersectionality has become a widespread and celebrated concept in gender and feminist studies, and finally also in the social sciences.

2.1 Constituent Parts of Intersectionality

2.1.1 A Definition - Inter-sectional-ity

Inter – is a prefix, occurring in loanwords from Latin, where it meant "among", "between", "in the midst of", "mutually", "reciprocally", "altogether" and "during"; used in
the formation of compound words.

Sectional(-ity) – is an adjective, and defines the composing of several independent
sections; (- ity) is the prefix.

As a noun, it suggests the point of contact made between categories, elements and lines. Intersectionality is a framework, consisting of the interconnected nature of social categorizations like class, gender, ability, ethnicity and race as they are
applied to a given individual group, considered as creating systems of disadvantage
or discrimination which are interdependent and overlapping. As a result, we can better acknowledge the differences among us through an awareness of the term intersectionality.

As an analytical tool, the main focus lies on the subjects that assume the posi-
tions of such intersections. The aim is to further feminist's agenda to not merely a focus on gender as the origin of female oppression, but to expand their energies for
studying other dimensions of power, such as the social categorizations as mentioned

4

above. Since multiple notions of intersectionality exist, its expansive character is reflected.

As a field of research, it is the study of overlapping or, in this case, intersecting social identities and also related systems of discrimination, domination and oppression. It is a theory that suggests but also seeks to examine how various cultural, social and biological categories such as class, ability, gender, race, religion, age, nationality and other axes of identity interact on these multiple axes and simultaneous levels.

As a theory, the proposal is to think that each trait or element of an individual person is inseparable linked with all other elements in order to understand one's identity in full. This can be used to get an understanding of how systematic injustice and social inequality appear on the multidimensional levels. All different concepts of oppression within society do not act independently of each other. It has always been this way, even though the term intersectionality came to the forefront of sociological circles in the late 1960's.

2.1.2 Historical Background: Intersectionality

The concept of intersectionality is understood to come to the foreground of sociological circles at the end of the 1960s and the early 1970s in connection with the multiracial feminist movement. Radical feminism that had evolved in the late 1960s, known as "re-visionist feminist theory", was criticized and the term intersectionality came as a part of that critique. This theory questioned the notion that gender was the main factor determining the fate of women. This investigation showed a historical exclusion of women of color from the feminist movement and the knowledge that they have long been excluded from the civil rights movement.

Through an introduction of the intersectional theory, women of color were supported to make claims that they do belong in both of these political spheres. Moving in these spheres, women of color were against the idea that women can be seen as a homogeneous category who share equal life experiences. The movement stemmed from the insight that white middle-class women do not function as the one and only representation of the feminist movement. Consequently, white middle-class women were recognized to have experienced different forms of oppression than those of black, poor, or disabled women. Henceforward, feminists sought to grasp the ways in which class, race and gender are combined to "determine the female destiny" (Hooks, 10).

> Every women's movement in America from its earliest origin to the present day has been built on racist foundation – a fact which in no way invalidates feminism as a political ideology. The racial apartheid social structure that characterized 19th and early 20th century American life was mirrored in the women's rights movement. The first white women's rights advocates were never seeking social equality for all women; they were seeking social equality for white women (bell hooks, 391)

The term intersectionality can also be linked historical and theoretical to the concept of 'simultaneity'. During the 1970s members of the 'Combahee River Collective', a group of black lesbian feminists in Boston, Massachusetts brought up the subject. They were early articulators of multiple oppressions experienced by women of color and these were the core shaped by simultaneous influences of class, sexuality, gender and race. The name of the Collective was taken from the guerilla action led by Harriet Tubman in 1863, in the Port Royal of South Carolina. More than 750 slaves were freed through this action, which is the only military campaign in the US history planned and led by women (Bridge, 210). The Women of the Collective, thus pushed forward the understanding of African American's experiences that challenged analyzes, resulting from black but also from male-centered social movements and furthermore; those from mainstream white, middle-class and heterosexual feminists.

Fast forward to 1989, Kimberlé Crenshaw described through the concept of intersectuality the ways in which the institutions of oppression and discrimination are interconnected and cannot be analyzed separately from one another. As for her theory, it can be said, in other words, that certain groups of women have to deal with multi-layered facets in their lives: "If Black women were free, it would mean that everyone else would have to be free since our freedom would necessitate the destruction of all the systems of oppression" (Bridge, 215).

2.1.3 Class, Race, Gender

Since the social, cultural and biological categories are defining a person, it is important to understand what is meant by the terms of their constituents. All times, the human existence is determined by a multicultural society; groups and individuals who identify themselves and live within the context of their race, class, gender, and ethnicity. To get a deeper understanding of the following film-and book-analyzes in terms of intersectionality, these terms deserve more detail consideration.

2.1.3.1 Race

Race is a socially defined reality and not a biological one (DNA evidence from Human Genome Project). Categories of race are the base for assigning social resources and different distributions of power, prestige and privilege. There exists a so called 'racial formation' which describes the phenomena of a continually creation and formation of racial categories, for instance African American, Hispanic or Asian American. Race is also used to socially identify groups based on physical distinctions. Ethnicity determines distinctive national origin, culture and religion. Further, racial-ethnic groups are socially subordinated and still remain culturally distinct within the United States.

2.1.3.2 Class

A status hierarchy in which groups and individuals are classified on the basis of prestige and esteem obtained primarily through economic success and the collection of wealth. Social classes can also refer to any special level in such a hierarchy. Many societies are recognized through four common social classes which are (1) upper class (2) Middle class (3) Working class and (4) Lower class. Several different dimensions of social class exist, including income, wealth, power, education, occupation, race and ethnicity. A cultural explanation of class would be that each class is viewed as having a distinctive culture but some societies are still based on the structure of social class where everything they can and will do in their life, is dictated by the class they are born into.

2.1.3.3 Gender

Like race and class, gender is a basic ordering principle of society. The basis for treating women and men differently are social as well as cultural definitions of femininity and masculinity, like dividing labor, allocation of social rewards or assigning roles. The system of gender, is denying both, women and men, a full range of social and human possibilities. Gender exceeds class and racial divisions. In comparison, the term 'sex' denotes biologically determined, and therefore the unchangeable difference between men and women.

3 12 years a slave

The 1853 memoir, autobiography and slave narrative *12 years a slave* recounts Solomon Northup's life story as a free black man who was born in New York state in the North, kidnapped and sold into slavery in the pre-Civil War South. He was the son of an emancipated slave and lived, worked, and married in upstate New York, where he resided with his family. He was a talented violin player and a multifaceted laborer. In 1841, he was tricked by two men who offered him profitable work in a circus playing the fiddle. Northup had confidence in them and followed the two con men to Washington D.C, where he was drugged, kidnapped, and afterwards sold as a slave into the Red River region of Louisiana. In the next twelve years kept in bondage, he survived as the human property of several different slave masters, and at last and for long ten years, under the cruel and tyranny ownership of a southern planter namely Edwin Epps. Northup succeeded to write a letter to friends and family in New York, who in turn rescued him with the aid of the state and he was finally freed in January 1853. After his return he wrote his account with the help of the editor David Wilson, and thus provides extensive details on slave markets in Washington D.C and New Orleans and further provides at length cotton and sugar cultivation but above all, the treatment of slaves on major plantations in Louisiana. Major thematic topics of both, the book and the film, are slavery as a moral cancer, freedom, injustice, the inherent dignity of all humanity, religion and slavery, man's inhumanity to man, slavery's toll on servant and master alike, and the place of women in society.

3.1 Historical background of 12 years a slave

3.1.1 The American Pre - Civil War

To understand the treatment of slaves during this time, the historical background will help examine the predominant political and social situation the people lived in. The United States fought from 1861 to 1865 in the American Civil War, Solomon Northup's story took place in the setting of the pre-Civil War South and had its origin in the issue of slavery. In the time of the American Revolution (1775-83), "the status of a slave had been institutionalized as a racial caste associated with African ancestry" (Field, 1995). In 1789, the United States Constitution was ratified and a fairly small number of free people of color were among citizens able to vote. Abolitionist laws, who were against slavery, were passed in most Northern states during and following the Revolutionary War. A movement developed to abolish slavery.

According to contemporary actors, fighting soldiers, the Union and Confederate leadership, slavery caused the Civil War. Union men believed the war functioned to emancipate the slaves; Confederates fought to protect southern society, and slavery as a part of it (Eskridge, 2011). From an anti-slavery perspective, the issue was mainly about if the system of slavery was an evil that was not compatible with Republicanism. In the U.S. Containment the strategy of anti-slavery forces was to stop an expansion and thus to terminate it.

In the South, however, slave-holding interests condemned this strategy as abusive upon their Constitutional rights (Chadwick, 2016). Whites from the South believed that the emancipation of slaves would ruin the economy because of the supposed laziness of blacks under free labor. In the North, slavery was illegal and has been outlawed in the late 18th and the early 19th Century. In the Southern cities this ban was faded and slavery expanded in highly profitable cotton districts of the South and Southwest.

4 12 years a slave – The Narrative of Solomon Northup

> Twelve Years a Slave (1853) is a memoir and slave narrative by Solomon
> Northup. Northup, a black man who was born free in New York, details his
> kidnapping in Washington, D.C. and subsequent sale into slavery. After hav-
> ing been kept in bondage for 12 years in Louisiana by various masters,
> Northup was able to write to friends and family in New York, who were able
> to secure his release. (Wilson)

The book consists of 22 chapters and covers five primary periods in the life of Solomon Northup:

1. Solomon Northup as a free man
2. Solomon Northup as a captive
3. Solomon Northup as a slave
4. Solomon Northup as a slave under Edwin Epps
5. Solomon Northup as a free man again

The fourth phase of Solomon Northup's *12 years a slave* is narrated in Chapters
XII-XX, focusing on the ten year bondage under the tyranny of his final and cruelest
master Edwin Epps, who whipped his slaves almost daily. Northup describes the
harsh daily circumstances he experienced on two different plantations of Edwin
Epps, including abuse, humiliation, and deprivation for all slaves living there.

Employing the concept of intersectionality, the two most tragic female figures of
12 years a slave will be examined, and related to the constituents of the term. On the
one hand, both women are presented in the framework of intersectionality in an exact
same manner of being oppressed, on the other hand, it is remarkable how different
these similar conditions are lived out due to of the circumstances in those days.

4.1 Deploying intersectionality

4.1.1 Mistress Epps – the green-eyed monster

Mary Epps is the well-educated wife of Edwin Epps and originates from a re-
spected family. Very much like Edwin Epps, she is illustrated as a racist, sadistic,
cold-hearted, malicious and selfish person. However, she treats the majority of her
husband's slaves well, with the exception of Patsey. Patsey incurs Mary Epps bot-
tomless hatred due to Edwin Epps' affection. Therefore, Mary Epps may be consid-

ered as a woman that occupies a position of racial privilege, while she is oppressed on a gender-basis.

In particular, the situation when Master Epps, his wife and Patsey act inside the Epps building shows strong evidence of intersectionality, concerning gender roles: "Mistress Epps made her claim as a woman by handling Patsey with aggression and no mercy due to the infidelity of her husband. Although Mistress Epps was the authority in the domestic sphere, she still was no more than property to Master Epps" (Northup, 107). Moreover, Mr. Epps' statement that he is willing to send her back to where he picked her up if she dares to expel Patsey, indicates the complicated occurrences of intersections between race, gender and power in the Old South. Additionally, it is pointed out that Mistress Epps, as an esteemed woman, acts "high and mighty, but held little real power" in such a patriarchal society (75).

Regarding the position of racial privilege, she also acts in conformity with her sensitive side. Northup writes she "was not naturally such an evil women, after all. She was possessed of the devil, jealousy, it is true, but aside from that, there was much in her character to admire" (76). For instance, when she argues in favor of Solomon's defense when Mr. Epps tried to attack Solomon with a knife to cut his throat: "In other situations—in a different society from that which exists on the shores of Bayou Boeuf, she would have been pronounced an elegant and fascinating woman," (76). Traditionally, white middle-class women have been treated as delicate and overly emotional – with the destiny to subordinate themselves to white men. There are numerous indications that Mary suffers from her destiny, and that it is not only her fault how she mistreats Patsey due to the existing social occurrences at that time, because "black women have been denigrated and subject to the racist abuse that is a foundational element of US society" (Crenshaw, 91).

While experiencing many forms of oppressions Mary undergoes, there is also the downside, when she is inflicting pain and suffer on Patsey, the black innocent girl. Mrs. Epps insists that Edwin punishes Patsey with frequent deprivations and whippings because she was unable to convince him to sell her; "he would whip her, merely to gratify the mistress" (75). Since it was Mary's only pleasure in life, turning Patsey's life in a living hell, Mary would physically humiliate and assault Patsey whenever she had the chance: "The pride of the haughty woman was aroused; the blood of the fiery southern boiled at the sight of Patsey, and nothing less than trampling out the life of the helpless bondwoman would satisfy her" (99). Again, it be-

11

comes clear in which form Mary's suffering is expressed; by being cruel: Patsey had become "the slave of a licentious master and a jealous mistress [...] the enslaved victim of lust and hate" (105) with nothing delighting the Mistress more than seeing Patsey suffer.

Furthermore, there is a twisted relationship between the two main female characters Patsey and Mistress Epps, which is characterized by different forms of oppression and inequality overlapping in multidimensional ways. According to McCall, intersectionality addresses "the relationships among multiple dimensions and modalities of social relations and subject formations". Both have to survive the demonic conditions of American slavery in their own ways, personifying black and white women's painful slave burden. On the one hand, there is Patsey who seems to be double enslaved by virtue of her beauty and her race. In an "almost human moment", when she is dancing because Solomon is singing violin, all of a sudden she goes down, knocked out by a heavy crystal decanter hurled at her head which is thrown by the Mistress. By this, Mistress Epps made her again the inferior black woman she was before, lying down on the floor. On the other hand, Edwin Epps is addicted to Patsey what makes the mistress full of hate and Patsey to a disease for her but Epps refuses his wife, humiliates her and claims that he has the desire for the puddle of "nasty nigger wench at their feet" (69). The relationship between the two female's characters is marked by these multiple forms of oppression and discrimination which are interacting and overlapping with each other and influence the treatment of the two women in multiple ways.

4.1.2 Patsey – the helpless bondwoman

The enslaved African-American woman lived in the mid of the 19th century and is the 23 year old slave of Edwin Epps. She is the most tragic figure in *12 years a slave*. Her mother was from Guinea, also enslaved and taken to Cuba and later sold to a family in the Southern region of the United States. Patsey "[...] is the offspring of a "Guinea nigger", brought over to Cuba in a slave ship, and in the course of trade transferred to Buford, who was her mother's owner" (Northup, 71). It is believed that Patsey have been born in South Carolina around 1830, and that she was sold to Edwin Epps when she was 13.

When Northup arrived on Epps plantation, they developed a close friendship. This led him to write about her and the psychological as well as physical nature of slavery's brutality. He describes her naturally "a joyous creature, a laughing, light-hearted girl, rejoicing in the mere sense of existence" (72). Patsey is seen as "the simpleminded slave, in whose heart God had implanted the seeds of virtue" (76). She was the fastest and most productive cotton picker on Epps's plantation, *the queen of the fields*. Therefore, he refused to sell her despite his wife's constant demands in that regard. Patsey was unlike all the other slaves because she had "a sense of spirit unwavering in its strength" and had been admired for her unique "sprightliness and pleasant disposition" (75). When Epps started assaulting and raping her, she would have been under 18. As soon as, Epps' wife, Mary, realized the ravishments of her husband, she became jealous at Patsey and began to beat and abuse her.

The frequent cruelties made Patsey despondent and suicidal as the years went on, "she had been literally excoriated" (77). The intense brutality she suffered from "a licentious master and a jealous mistress" (74) drove her wish to death. Once, she turned to Solomon begging him to end her life. This happened when she had the "favor" of Epps at that time, meaning that Patsey is the subject to an endless stream of abuse and inhuman conditions from his wife and frequent sexual assaults through his hands.

Patsey is a very pitiful character. As mentioned above, she has an admirable character but due to the fact that she is colored and born as a slave, she has to labor under the disadvantages to which her unfortunate race is subjected. Patsey, also known as *the Queen of the fields,* picks five hundred pounds of cotton a day, in contrast to Solomon, who is not able to harvest more than two hundred per day. She does not do it for reasons of loyalty, but it is a living delight in her own quickness, just as with the dance. Solomon writes that he has "not the gift – the dexterous fingers and quick motion of Patsey, who could fly along one side of a row of cotton, stripping it of its undefiled and fleecy whiteness miraculously fast" (68). This information indicates that "Patsey would surely have been beaten if she failed to produce twice as much" (62). She is described as a "splendid animal" and that she would have been chief among many of her people; of her race, if her intellect would not have been enshrouded in slavery's darkness. Through experiencing the differences of class, race, gender and ethnicity; her fate treated her unkindly.

One of the most meaningful and significant incidents in *12 years a slave*s, may represent nearly every form of oppression and violence a person can suffer from. One day, when Patsey visits Harriet, the wife of an acquaintance of Epps, to ask for a bar soap because the Mistress won't allow her to have any, she gets into big trouble. When she returns, Epps does not believe her and is furious, thinking her guilty of a sexual encounter with the white master of another plantation. Solomon is forced to deliver the lashings to the helpless and naked girl who screams for mercy "oh mercy, massa! – oh! have mercy, *do*. Oh, God! pity me," (100), while Edwin and Mistress Epps goaded him on, and the flesh of Patsey is quivering at every stroke: "Mistress Epps stood on the piazza among her children, gazing on the scene with an air of heartless satisfaction [and] the lash was wet with blood, which flowed down her sides and dropped upon the ground" (100).For Solomon it was "the most cruel whipping that [he] ever was doomed to witness—one [he] can never recall with any other emotion than that of horror"(102). Patsey was literally flayed from over 40 lashes but that was not enough for Epps – after Northup throws down the whip, refusing to go any further, he picked it up and applied it with "ten-fold" greater force than Northup had. After this experience Patsey and Solomon were severely traumatized and will never forget what happened. The characters of Patsey and Solomon experienced many forms of oppression. Especially Patsey, as the victim of the whipping, seems to portray the tragic but heroic figure of enslaved black women who had no chance to break out the system. This scenery also shows how slavery systematically stripped the bondsmen of all hope due to the psychological brutality of the system. Since the times of slavery, Black women have eloquently described the multiple oppressions of race, class, and gender—referring to the concept of intersectionality as "interlocking oppressions," "simultaneous oppressions," "double jeopardy," "triple jeopardy" or any number of descriptive terms (Crenshaw, 108).

4.1.3 From white to black; from men to women and back - Bringing it together

As delineated above, considering race, gender, ethnicity and class, American slavery was an insidious institution of the economy, developed to benefit a minority of white Christian men, always trying to prevent others access or ability to establish coalitions. White women are privileged with no real power and no position; but powerful with no promise of independence, loyalty or safety. In general, black women are branded as sub-human and inferior. The next level down - black enslaved women, just like Patsey - controlled and terrorized by white women like Mrs. Epps. Both parties cannot rage against white males' supremacy. Therefore, Mistress Epps as an "evil woman" can be understand as a white women bound in slavery, being in a tumultuous rage, whilst black women were raped, disgraced and discarded after, without any authority. According to Crenshaw, the latter are discriminated both, as women and as blacks.

Apart from men's power over women in general, black and white American women were doomed through the introduction of asymmetric, maliciously competitive, treacherous and inhuman deranging circumstances. As to the historic perspective, the women were systematically cultured to mistrust and envy each other. In the historic role of slavery and racial segregation in the United States, all women are oppressed as women, but race and class must have been central aspects to these deranging circumstances. They are laying the cornerstone for different axes of intersectionality, and also the myriad of circumstances under which enslaved women had to live. The solidarity of black women, especially enslaved black women, seemed to be reason enough for deploying the issues of intersectionality's constituents. Being black, female and enslaved; or being white, male or female is the anchor point of exploring how identity can impact one's life.

While experiencing many of these impacts, Crenshaw emphasizes the importance of Sojourner Truth's famous speech "Ain't I a woman?" which can be applied to the conditions of Patsey and Mistress Epps living as discriminated women. Mary Epps for instance, decisively explores the complicated position of white women within racialist capitalist patriarchal power structures which were happening in the context of the 19th Century in terms of sexist oppression and racial privilege. It is clear that she is powerless what makes her more sensitive to the struggles of her slaves and she behaves just as cruel as her husband toward them, and especially toward Patsey. While ploughing and laboring twice as much as any men on the cotton field, Patsey should have been allowed to eat as much as a man – if she could get it. But this was not the case. Undeserved, she beared about 50 lashes, more than any slave Solomon had ever seen (112). Enslaved women lived like beasts and the "free" women behaved like savages. The words of *Ain't I a woman?* contrast the character of oppression faced by white and colored women. Witnessing Mary, indicates very much on the idea that white women occupy a position of racial privilege even though they were clearly oppressed on a gender-basis. According to this privilege, they can act just as bad as their white male counterparts. Therefore, *12 years a slave* can serve as an approach to intersectionality and its constituents showing dif-

15

ferent forms of social inequality, oppression and discrimination which are overlapping and interacting with each other in multiple ways.

5   12 years a slave – The Film

In 2013, Solomon Northup's slave narrative memoir was adapted to the cinema screen by screenwriter John Ridley and director Steve McQueen, known primarily for *Hunger* (2008) and *Shame* (2011). In addition to many other honors, *12 years a* slave won three Academy Awards, including Best Adapted Screenplay, Best Picture, and Best Supporting Actress for Lupita Nyong'o, who played Patsey. The novel is considered a major success. The film also became an international blockbuster. Hollywood's finest actors such as Michael Fassbender or Brad Pitt starred in this film. The movie itself performed well above the expectation and received a particularly extraordinary review.

The film is oriented at Northup's memoir, including some original phrases from the book. However, the film adaption of Solomon Northup's bestseller is, obviously not as accurate with factual detail as the book was, resulting in shortcuts of storytelling and a "muddying of facts that are often found in book-to-film adaptions" (The Root). For instance, a slave trader namely Goodin is completely eliminated from the story in the blockbuster movie, along with Solomon's experience in his possession. Moreover, the two slaves Clemens Ray and Arthur are combined into one character, and Northup's time with William Ford, a white "noble, candid, Christian man" (Northup, 24) is abridged. Just like Solomon's real-life experience, a large part of the film version takes part on Epps' plantation and concerns itself primarily with Patsey's sorrows. In that regard, it is close to the memoir, which focuses explicitly – as the film – on the black women's personal story. Still it ignores other significant events that happened in the book, for example other stories of male slaves such as Abram or Wiley.

In addition, in Northup's memoir, he narrates that he has been forced to be the slave-whipping driver for eight years. The film, however, omits this considerable fact, expect of one short scene, in which Northup gives Patsey a brutal whipping. In fact, it makes the film scene more crucial and emotional, and, further is probably the biggest discrepancy with regard to the real story. Solomon was forced by Mr. Epps and cheered by his jealous wife to whip Patsey. In the book, it was only the Mistress who wants to bribe Solomon to kill Patsey. This would have shown more clearly how immense the Mistress' oppression on Patsey was, and how much her husband, as a white male, influenced her behaving towards the black enslaved girl. By omitting the fact, that this was not Solomon's only whipping against like-minded slaves, the importance of gender, race and ethnicity is highlighted very much because of emphasizing the power relations between the actors and their status.

Some criticized that the success of the film is based on its extensive depiction of cruelty, agony and inhumanity. Indeed, it is depressing for the cinema visitors, who attended the film because of portraying America's distressing slave history. Additionally, it has been said that "overall, the movie *12 Years a Slave* does a better-than-average job of portraying the content of its source material, but there are too many creative licenses taken in the film to trust it as a reliable substitute for reading Northup's memoir" (New York Times). While it is not the role of reviewers to tell people which films to see and which to avoid, *12 years a slave* definitely is a very powerful film confronting with the grim reality of slavery in a very special way that has never been done before. It is a film of blunt emotional trauma which helps reviewers and moviegoers understand the emotional realities of America's history in all of its cruelty and the limitations on its kindness.

During McQueen's speech at the Oscar ceremony, he underlined the importance of Solomon Northup's narration, especially for the women who endured slavery, no matter if they were black or white: "The last word: everyone deserves not just to survive, but to live. This is the most important legacy of Solomon Northup. I dedicate this award to all the people who have endured slavery, especially to women in slavery. And the 21 million people who still suffer slavery today. Thank you very much. Thank you." (McQueen). Hence, it became clear how much all the different axes of intersectionality and its constituents were involved in the production of the film. Camera work, composition, film editing, art direction, film style, as well as music and sound did a significant job in constituting them, interacting and overlapping with each other.

In the following section, I will elaborate on the meanings and effects created through cinematographic techniques and elements which are deploying the concept of intersectionality.

5.1 Film style

Film style, refers more to the overall impression of a film in relation to reality. Most movies are in line with what may be defined as the classical Hollywood cinema style, adhering strongly to the principles of reality and establishing continuity in narrative, time and space.

McQueen asserted that he has no distinct style in *12 years a slave*. However, critics have identified recurring tropes, such as the daringly lengthy single takes which appear talismanic. At a deeper level, there is a consistent interest in the punishment of bodies in McQueen's films, like in *Hunger* and in *Shame*. "That unflinching gaze is McQueen's signature move, as viewers of his first two features, the Bobby Sands biopic Hunger and the sex-addiction drama Shame, will already know" (The Telegraph). Bodies are variously starved, beaten or entangled.

For instance, one scene is deliberately intense in the way it is constructed regarding the representative time span it covers, its visual elements as well as the way the different shots are edited together. Northup is strung up on a cypress tree, his tiptoes slip in the mud underfoot, his throat is stretched long by the noose, and his breath comes in shallow clucks. This happens, while life on the plantation behind him runs it normal course. At this stage of *12 years a slave,* the audience expects that the scene quickly cuts into the next one which would bring Northup's fate to a dramatic conclusion – either he will be rescued, or he dies. As already mentioned, by being a Steve McQueen film, the scenery does not what is expected by the audience, but rather, the camera remains on Solomon Northup who is continuing to struggle for his life for more than 3 minutes in the movie. Therefore, it can be said that visually intense and lengthy takes are a signature characteristic in McQueen's films.

Going further with the film style, the employed narrative structure is simple and coherent. The camera moves in a very natural, realistic way and rarely assumes standpoints that deviate from the normal perception of the world.

> One of the major demands is to create a visual consistency over extended periods. You are basically compressing time, and making it believable, so people don't see the artifice in a half-day's filming that ends up as six minutes on screen. We wanted to create something that felt real and accurate, so that at no point is the audience taken out of the film itself — so that the world we created has verisimilitude, that there is a truth to it, to heighten the impact of Solomon's story (Bobbit).

5.2 Music and Sound

Music can play an essential role in film production, establishing, underlining and characterizing the main themes and character constellations of the film narrative. Film music further helps to "transform the cinematic image-event into an affect image-event" (Brown, 28). Similar to the other cinematic techniques employed in *12 years a slave,* music and sound primarily serve the purpose of enhancing the drama, amplifying the emotions of the characters, and creating an emotional effect upon the audience. The musical score to *12 years a slave* was composed by Hans Zimmer, a famous German composer and multiple award winner: "Music can actually make you cry. I don't mean that like a horrible, manipulative thing, but music can get at parts of your psyche that other things can't get at [...] I try to do something that resonates very quickly and takes you on a journey" (Zimmer).

His film score was challenged to depict a black, and also a white world that oscillates between these two extreme poles in the screenplay, for example, the rapes, physical and psychological tortures, horrific mutilations on the one side; and the everyday – eating, backbreaking work, and sex on the other. One instance is, when Patsey gets beaten down by Mary Epps, because she was dancing to music in a circle of other enslaved black men and women who have been roused from slumber in the middle of the night, to dance a jig, play music, and entertain their owner Edwin Epps. This scene employs the concept of amplifying emotions of the characters, and creating an emotional effect upon the audience.

In *12 years a slave* no "sentimental music" is implemented, while sex is mostly depicted to function for tyranny or presenting a context of some kind of control: painful, horrible and enforced. Thus sound and music are used to underline the circumstances under which black and white slaves had to live at that time, and create identification with different characters, with all their fears, emotions, and particularly the grief, concerning their destiny as a slave.

To sum it up, music and sound hence underline the characters' feelings and emotions, aiming at eliciting an emotional response from the spectators, forcing them into an active stance rather than passively involving them.

5.3 Camera Work

Camera work generally describes the shot the camera assumes. It incorporates aspects like focal length, camera angles and viewpoints. With regard to focal length, it is distinguished between long distance shots, medium shots and close-up shots. Whilst long and medium shots are used to introduce the audience to the scenery and the characters, close-up shots are primarily used to convey feelings and emotions. A change in the focal length is referred to as zoom. Whereas zoom-ins evoke the impression of moving towards an object, zoom-outs create the feeling of moving away from an object. The camera angle marks the position of the camera in relation to the object. Here, it is primarily distinguished between high angle and low angle shots, bird's eye view and worm's eye view shots. Viewpoints then combine both elements: focal length and camera angles. Examples include the eye-level shot and the point of view shot. Generally, the way the camera is adjusted can affect the viewers' perception of the object and can elicit different emotions.

In *12 years a slave,* the camera work is one of the primary means of conveying viewpoints. Of course, Solomon's perspective and view of the world predominates in the film, but through one of McQueen's most important techniques using lengthy static takes, important key moments are communicated, via the narration, but also in terms of camera work. Extended shots are frequently employed throughout the entire film to convey Solomon's perspective. Crucial for this style of filmmaking, is the usage of a single camera setup. Extended shots, made with a single camera, are

> the most efficient and effective because [they] make you concentrate, instead of just hoovering up a bunch of images and finding the scene in the edit. You have to make decisions on the day itself, and that really sharpens everyone. For me that's kind of the essence of filmmaking (Bobbit).

Taking, for example, the scene where Northup burns the letter he was writing to be smuggled home to his family - this shot of a burning letter away into the deep night, is one of the film's most visually resonant moments. For the audience, the image of the letter burning away is made to be a ravishing one and heartbreaking by the knowledge of what the content is. By using such camera work, the audience can built its own viewpoint, but in fact, the degradation of slaves and other constituents of intersectionality are employed subconsciously. The camera insistently assumes Solomon's viewpoints, primary conveying his feelings and emotions towards the external word, and emphasizes the inhuman circumstances slaves had to survive. The following examples are illustrative of such shots.

5.3.1 The whipping

Moving in to or out of a medium or close-up shot, is commonly known as zooming. There are several instances in *12 years a slave* where the camera utilizes this feature. At the climax of the film, for instance, where Solomon is forced to whip Patsey, the camera zooms out of an extreme close-up on Patsey, effectively introducing the character's suffering to the audience. As the camera zooms out, the intense emotion of the scene is illustrated by displaying Epps, Solomon and Patsey because:

> This scene is the culmination of all the humiliation, pain and fear and all the degradation, when he's forced to whip the one person he has a connection with, someone he loves. It's heartbreaking, so it was crucial for that scene to work with this camera work (McQueen)

The camera gets right into the moment by capturing every of the 50 strokes of the whip on Patsey's bleeding back. When zooming in, the camera focuses, again with that discomfort lengthy shot, on her mangled back, and then zooms out slowly to display the full dimension of this scene. By zooming in and out, this close-up represents the journey of twelve years a slave of Solomon, projected on Patsey's back. It functions like a reminder what really happened in the past, and the audience is confronted with that fact through McQueen's camera work.

5.4 Editing

Film editing generally refers to the post-production process of selecting and combining shots into sequences. It describes the relationship between shots and the process by which they are combined. Therefore, editing incorporates the creative and meaningful assemblage of images, dialogue, music and pacing, usually following specific principles and conventions. Moreover, it is crucial to the creation of narrative space and the establishment of narrative time and is essential in establishing the overall feeling of a film.

Concerning the interlinking of sequences, the film disobeys the rules of traditional Hollywood continuity editing, by not establishing smooth transitions between the scenes. A good illustration for this is the whipping scene in the movie. It is an extended shot and, hence, it magnifies the use of violence in this particular film scene. By extending a shot and not editing it, the audience sticks to the scene. The contrary would result in reminding the audience subconsciously that they are watching a film that is not real, and they start to relax. Thus, if there is no edit, the audience gets no chance to relax and is drawn deeper into the emotion of the scene itself. "The editing and cinematography makes the audience feel like they are constantly circling him, like the slaves behind, wanting to do something to help but unable to leave their seats" (Clay).

5.5 Art Direction

Art direction or production design generally refers to the overall visual and auditory design of a film and includes various different aspects such as set design, lighting and colors, as well as costumes and props. Such elements may be considered quite fundamental as the "visual ambiance of the film may enhance its emotional dimensions, nonverbally further the plot, draw character profiles, and in enumerable ways add to the content of the film" (Heisner, 2).

The setting of *12 years a slave* is Louisiana and embraces a number of different effects the cinematographer and producer of the film used efficiently. According to Sean Bobbit, the two guiding principles for the cinematography of *12 years a slave* are simplicity and beauty. These principles manifest themselves in the shooting of the film and build an approach to the issue of intersectionality, together with a counterpoint to the on-screen violence. Oftentimes, films which contain a lot of violence, like in *12 years a slave,* are shot in a way where cinematography itself mirrors the violence and function as an invaluable cinematic tool. In the case of *12 years a slave,* the approach takes the opposite, Bobbitt and McQueen:

> [...] utilized the natural beauty of Louisiana, coupled with an utterly beautiful filming style, and used this beauty as a counterpoint to the on-screen violence, and as a brief respite from the film's many emotionally devastating moments. It's an odd juxtaposition (violence and beauty), but one that actually benefits the film in many ways

Regarding the plantation of Edwin Epps, there were no rose gardens unlike the beautiful Louisiana shown before. McQueen opted for a pigsty in the background. "It's a much harder place," he said. "The color is somewhat drained out. It's not as lush. The earth is dustier." The outhouses are constructed rougher and more slaves are crowded into them. At the beginning, the whipping post which is next to the pigsty, is not noticed by the camera until its finally use in the brutal whipping scene of Patsey. By changing the setting to Epps unpleasant and ominous plantation, his power and the difference in gender roles, race, and ethnicity is highly emphasized.

Lighting primarily serves to establish the melancholic atmosphere of the film. Dim lighting is frequently employed in the scenes focusing upon the sad subject of the film, adding a somber atmosphere of the film as a whole. In *12 years a slave* the whole set is lighted, so the actors and also the camera can be free within the space, and 360° shots are possible by having the light come through the windows or from top-lights. As delineated above, simplicity and beauty are the two principles of the film, and that is why it is kept simple with lighting and the actors can play with the atmosphere: "Sometimes they tend to play just near the light, and sometimes they will find the darker space in the room, if you got it wrong you have to be very quick and your gaffer is your best friend" (Bobbitt).

By using this technique, the film has an immense dynamic range, for example, in emotional scenes; the characters' faces are molded with caressing, soft-toned light, enhancing the emotional effect. The light symbolizes power and is in the possession of the white man Edwin Epps. He has control over Northup whose head and eyes are facing downward in vulnerability. The light is natu-ral and not made artificial. It is placed in a position to show the interrogation of Solo-mon who is helplessly trying to talk his way out of slaughter. Lighting hence has ef-fective means to establish the feeling of reality and the contrast between black and white skin color within nighttime and daytime.

6   Conclusion: From Truthful Novel to Emotional Film

In this academic paper, I have examined two different media approaching inter-sectionality and its constituents in literary terms: Solomon Northup's slave narrative memoir *12 years a slave* and Steve McQueen's film adaption. First and foremost, I started to discover the term "intersectionality", which was coined by Kimberlé Cren-shaw. In fact, it was very important for me to impart knowledge about the word con-struction, to reveal its history and, further, its purport. Afterwards, I have illustrated that *12 years a slave* played in a different timeframe than Crenshaw's concepts was established and therefore addressed the issue of slavery and its history within the time of the American Civil War what is important to understand why Crenshaw came up with her thoughts.

As demonstrated, the novel is the narration of Solomon Northup about his obser-vations as a slave as well as a freeman, especially concerning the circumstances the women had to live in. That gave me space for interpreting and analyzing the concept of intersectionality and to apply it to the different perspectives and insights he gave by his memoir. Whilst each of the characters are consumed by his or her own, indi-vidual trauma, the forms of oppression and discrimination also dovetail and overlap, thus offering a multitude of different perspectives. Thus, I took a closer look on the two main female characters Patsey and Mary Epps, and examined how they deploy the concept of intersectionality. Then, I collected the reasons for the differences be-tween men and women, white and black humans at that time in terms of the concept.

Not only the novel deploys the concept of intersectionality, but also the adopted film by Steve McQueen. At first, I compared the novel and the film with regard to its credibility and authenticity for the audience, and mentioned some instances for this. Taken as a whole, the groundwork and the editing of the novel adds to the under-standing and processing of the theory of intersectionality, and helps in the section about the film with interpreting its making of. Particularly, through the interlinkage of different film techniques, the representation of how intersectionality deploys the film, is presented and offers a multilateral approach.

Ultimately, I have demonstrated that where the film indulges in an array of differ-ent cinematograph techniques to offer a complex account of trauma and the different axes of intersectionality, the memoir in comparison to that draws on a simple, one-dimensional narrative that primarily helps to get the real insight and the detailed understanding of the history. Whilst the novel engages the readers, actively involving them in the reading process, the film accentuates on special events in the life of Solomon Northup, stimulating emotions, as well as achieving an active involvement. It becomes clear that novel and film offer two vastly different ways of approaching intersectionality, illustrating the visual incidents and traumatic experiences of black and white men and women from the deeply emotional but also extremely tough movie to watch; to the candid and truthful statement of facts in the novel of this dark period in history.

7 Works cited

12 Years a Slave. Dir. Steve McQueen. Perf. Chiwetel Ejifor, Michael Fassbender, Benedict Cumberbatch, Paul Diano, Lupita Nyong'o, Sarah Paulson, Brad Pitt, Alerie Woodard. River Road Entertainment, 2014. DVD.

Andersen, Margaret L., and Patricia Hill Collins. *Race, Class, and Gender: An Anthology*. Belmont, CA: Wadsworth Cengage Learning, 2013. Print.

Andersen, Margaret L., Thinking About Women: Sociological Perspectives on Sex and Gender, 3rd edition. Macmillian Publishing Company, 1993.

Brown, Royal S. *Overtones and Undertones: Reading Film Music*. Berkeley: U of California, 1994. Print.

Chadwick, F. E. (2016). ... *Causes of the civil war, 1859-1861*. United States: Palala Press.

Clay, Kat. "Kidnapped Shadows: The Cinematography of 12 Years A Slave." *Kat Clay*. Kat Clay, 16 Feb. 2014. Web. 25 Sept. 2016.

Collin, Robbie. "12 Years A Slave, Review: 'This, at Last, Really Is History Written with Lightning'" *The Telegraph*. Telegraph Media Group, 4 June 2016. Web. 28 Sept. 2016.

Hooks, Bell. *Feminist Theory: From Margin to Center* (3rd ed.). New York: Routledge, 2015. Print.

Edwards, Breanna. "Lupita Nyong'o Is Against Turning 12 Years a Slave Site Into Baseball Stadium." *The Root*. N.p., 28 Oct. 2014. Web. 27 Sept. 2016.

Eisenstein, Zillah. "The Combahee River Collective Statement." *The Combahee River Collective Statement*. THE COMBAHEE RIVER COLLECTIVE, 1977. Web. 23 Aug. 2016.

Eskridge, Larry. "After 150 Years, We Still Ask: Why this Cruel War'?" *Canton Daily Ledger*. N.p., 29 Jan. 2011. Web. 24 Aug. 2016.

Field, R. (1995). *African peoples of the Americas: From slavery to civil rights* (7th ed.). New York, NY: Cambridge University Press.

Northup, Solomon. *Twelve Years a Slave*. Ed. David Wilson. N.Y: Whitehall, 1853. Print.

Schworer, Simon. *Human Genome Project*. Place of Publication Not Identified: Grin Verlag, 2013. Print.

Selby, Jenn. "12 Years A Slave: Brad Pitt and Steve McQueen's Best Picture Oscars Acceptance Speech in Full." *The Independent*. Independent Digital News and Media, 03 Mar. 2014. Web. 25 Sept. 2016.